SAINT ANTHONY

A BIBLICAL ASCETIC

by: Fr Matthew the Poor

SAINT ANTHONY
A BIBLICAL ASCETIC

St Anthony: A Biblical Ascetic

COPYRIGHT © 2014
St. Shenouda Monastery

ST SHENOUDA MONASTERY
8419 Putty Rd,
Putty, NSW, 2330
Sydney, Australia

www.stshenoudamonastery.org.au

ISBN 13: 978-0-9873400-6-1

Contents

Saint Anthony: A Biblical Ascetic

"Know this, children, that all commandments are neither hefty nor troublesome, but rather a true light and everlasting joy to those who utterly obey them"

Saint Anthony – Letter 14

"Truly the life of Saint Anthony is a righteous model for ascetic life"

Saint Athanasius - The Life of Anthony

"The account of the life of Anthony by Athanasius, is in fact a monastic rule in the form of a narrative"

Saint Gregory the Theologian

Saint Anthony was able to obtain a luminous ascetic life through the Bible. Let us beseech the Almighty God to bestow on us spiritual insight and grace so that we may hold firm to the holy traditions that were kept by our great father of worldwide Christian ascetics.

The life received by St. Anthony is one that is precisely in accordance with the Bible, one which was aided by tremendous power from the Holy Spirit. His going out into the wilderness as an eighteen year old, to live in the mountains and parched deserts, was an expression of the measure of intense faith that filled the heart of Anthony, the young teen who was accustomed to living a lavish lifestyle. He was not hindered by the circumstances of his one and only orphan sister, or the allure of three hundred acres of land that promised a comfortable earthly life.

What was it that drew St. Anthony away from earthly pleasures and towards a life of monasticism? It was undoubtedly the Lord Jesus Christ's teaching in the Holy Bible. This was the only incentive that stirred the heart of the young Anthony and made him forsake the world entirely. He had no other motivation or goal to strive toward.

This is affirmed by Saint Athanasius in his book *the life of the saint Anthony*: "The Lord kept him for our benefit and the benefit of others that he may become an instructor on the ascetic life that he received from the Holy books." *Life of Anthony, 45*

Therefore, obeying the holy call to ascetic life was the only objective that stirred St. Anthony, without thought or examination, to embark on a life of asceticism, solitude and abandonment of the world.

Alternative attempts at justifying the motives for asceticism in the life of St. Anthony are thus far from accurate. This becomes even clearer as we recall his calling to the life of asceticism. When he entered the church, he heard the Lord saying: "If you want to be perfect, go, sell what you have and give to the poor, and you will have treasure in heaven; and come, follow Me" (Matt 19:21). He immediately departed from the church, gave up his family's land to the villagers then sold the rest of his belongings. He distributed the large sum of money accrued from the sale of his possessions amongst the needy, keeping only a small portion for his sister.

A short time later he entered the church once more and heard the Lord saying: "Do not worry about tomorrow." (Matt 6:34) St. Anthony could no longer delay his departure from the world; but rather went out, and gave the little that was left for his sister to the poor, and devoted himself to solitude.

And what were the consequences, of this boldness, love and obedience? This we come to hear in his final words to his disciples, as he concludes his call which he obeyed and completed, saying:

"I, the destitute, thank the Lord my God, and glorify His name, whom I have inclined to, and served with all my heart from my youth till now; for he has not forsaken me, but supported me and saved me." *Letters, 19*

From this it is clear that the ascetic life practiced by St. Anthony was a practical application of the Divine Sacred command, which the Holy Spirit inspired in his heart. We ought to beseech God to bring us to this same solid foundation, so that we may truly realise that there is no other motive for a true life of asceticism, except for obeying the gospel's command for the sake of Christ. Therefore fasting, prayer, vigilance, poverty, chastity, obedience, and any other monastic virtue, ought to be solely motivated by love for the Lord Jesus and desire to please His Good Father with full sincerity and submission:

"If one were to love God with all their heart, all their mind and all their strength they will attain the fear of God, and fear yields grief, and grief yields power, and so the soul bears fruit by this power...Therefore, attain for yourselves this power so that devils may fear you; and the labours (virtues) that you practice, may be less tiring, and godliness will become more appealing to you...For the sweetness of the love of God is more pleasant than honeycomb." *Letters, 9*

"I do not grow weary of remembering you in my supplication before God night and day, so that your devotion to God may be firm; and thus your virtues may be multiplied, your gaze fixed, and your discernment wise; and God shall grant you tremendous power" *Letters, 12*

Thus if the goal or motive is deviated from this foundation under any internal or external circumstances of the soul, then the ascetic life has wandered outside the confines of the Bible. It is no longer in accordance with the lives of the early fathers. The consequence of this is that it becomes estranged from the inspiration of the Holy Spirit, and is deemed not to be a sacred calling according to the will of God.

What Being Obedient to the Divine Commandment Meant for St. Anthony

"Anthony was famed, not because of any writings, nor earthly wisdom, nor his proficiency in any work, but for his devotion to serving God"

Life of Anthony, 93

Obedience to the commandment, as understood from the life of St. Anthony, and as he himself realised, is based on the understanding that it is a divine instruction. It is therefore not subject to debate, nor is it to be considered in light of the potential reward; but rather, it is as a statute which is to be obeyed with love and dedication.

The objective of fulfilling the commandment is not for the sake of the promised reward, but steered by the zeal, joy and fervour that the Holy Spirit bestows on one's heart by conforming it to the will of God. This is perfect asceticism.

In light of this, let us again examine the Lord's command to St. Anthony: "Go, sell what you have and give to the poor, and you will have treasure in heaven; and come, follow Me" (Matt 19:21). St. Anthony's aim was not to acquire treasure in heaven, but to simply obey the Lord's command joyfully. The motive for his asceticism was not the reward of obeying the commandment faithfully, but rather obedience to the commandment itself!

If St. Anthony's objective in selling his possessions was acquiring treasure in heaven, he would have been content in only selling his possessions. However, we find him the next day, upon hearing the call "do not worry for tomorrow," immediately forsaking the world and dedicating himself to ascetic worship.

In other words, St. Anthony brought himself and his entire life to a complete halt for the sake of obeying the Lord's statutes, making the target of his struggle toward a given virtue, another virtue. So he would persist in prayer to gain purity of heart, thus making his prayer more fervent and influential. Or he would humble himself to gain the aid of the Holy Spirit, and for his humility to become even greater, and so on. Hence his ascetic motive was virtue and he continually implored God's power and the aid of the Holy Spirit that his victory may be accomplished.

"Virtues are not far from you, but are for you and within you…And so, if we begin walking the path of righteousness earnestly, we must intensify our struggle, so that we may attain the virtues that are set before us… Because virtue is within us and arises from us, therefore willing it is all that is required from us, for it is written "the kingdom of God is within you" (Luke 17:21)." (Life of Anthony part 20, and Letter 4)

"I entreat you to abandon sensual desire, but rather observe stillness that the heavenly powers may abide within you, by the Grace of the Holy Spirit, and your labour is according to His will." *Letters, 8*

And so virtue remained the motive and incentive for St. Anthony, in his extraordinary asceticism; in fasting, unceasing prayer, constant vigilance, chastity, love, modesty and service. His life became a living gospel, because he did not deviate from his original goal of obeying the Lord's commands, and did not concern himself with the promised rewards to those who keep them. Furthermore, when the devils attempted to lure him into contemplating the reward of his asceticism he would rebuke them. St. Anthony felt that anticipating any reward was outside the realms of obeying the divine command.

"And so if the devils were to praise your asceticism and call you blessed, do not incline to them…For many a time they glorified me, and so I would admonish them by the Lord's name" *Life of Anthony, 34, 38*

The Holy Spirit guided St. Anthony in this life and path,

so that it could be a pure testimony of biblical faith, and a holy model of monasticism to the entire world. This focus on practising virtue is in itself considered a genuine reflection on the true spirit of asceticism, which is not of St. Anthony, but of the Holy Spirit. It reveals the key to the strength and grace that accompanied him all his life and paints for us an accurate image of Christian asceticism, which is founded upon obeying the Lord Jesus.

Whoever is content with obeying the Lord's command without consideration of any reward exemplifies a state of God-inspired asceticism. This person affirms the genuineness of his devotion to the Lord Jesus, which is out of true love for Him and obedience to His words. His obedience is not contingent on a reward, whether that is for a particular spiritual state, or a heavenly or earthly prize. Hence we hear St. Anthony proclaiming this reality to his children in his eighth letter saying:

"And so from now on I beseech my Lord for your sake night and day, that He may grant you His gifts that He has bestowed on me by His grace alone, and not because I am of merit, for this is the genuine treasure that the Lord has granted me." *Letters, 8*

"It is not fitting for us to pray in order to learn the future, or seek knowledge as a wage for our asceticism, but rather, let us pray so that the Lord may be an aid unto us.

As for those who place a certain reward as a goal or basis for their struggle, they unknowingly go beyond the person of the Lord Jesus and plunge away from the meaning of obeying the divine commandment. Their struggle is motivated by personal interest in attaining an individual desire and not for Christ's sake. Their obedience to the commandment is in hope of receiving a certain gift, or talent, and not in order to submit to the Lord." *Life of Anthony, 33*

This is evident when we examine the following verse in a new light; "He who humbles himself will be exalted" (Luke 18:14). For he who humbles himself in order to be exalted, cannot truly be humble, and is in fact not humble whatsoever, as his motive is exaltation. Therefore, despite carrying out the most difficult tasks, even unto death, whilst setting a certain reward as a basis for their struggle, they are yet to be considered submissive to God and will not be counted as fulfilling the commandments. Rather, they are submissive to their own egos, and fulfilling their own will. About this St Isaac the Syrian says: "He who humbles himself in order to be praised by men will be put to shame by God!"

For the humble is not raised by their humility, but it is God who raises the meek; and so one cannot gain the reward on the grounds of their own struggle! Therefore, in order to offer ascetic works that are according to God's will, they must only be for the sake of obeying God, and not for gaining a certain gift or reward.

Offering One's Entire Life to God is the Hidden Reason for the Strength of the Ascetic

"From now on, give neither rest to your eyes nor slumber to your eyelids, until you come to raise yourselves as pure sacrifices to the Lord and be made worthy to behold Him; for as the apostle says, without purity no one can perceive Him"

Letters, 5

"For this reason my beloved children, I do not grow weary of my supplications for you by night and day so that the Lord may grant you the spirit of discernment, so that you may offer yourselves up to God as acceptable living sacrifices"

Letters, 6

From St. Anthony's biography, we are able to perceive a clear directive for his bold, brave and dedicated ascetic works. It is simply that St. Anthony firmly set his heart on submitting and offering his life to God.

This directive, I mean offering one's life to God without regard for weakness or illness or death, was indeed the key to St. Anthony's ascetic practices. This is true of his boldness in dwelling in graves, or inhabiting the barren mountains amongst the wild beasts; or his valiant defiance of Satan, or his constant spiritual growth even in his elderly years. This was all done with no regard for people's ridicule, or the contempt of friends and family, along with utterly drowning any hope, or even the notion, of going back on surrendering life entirely to God.

"Thus if we have truly begun walking the path of righteousness, and persist in it, it is necessary for us to intensify our struggle... and not turn back as Lot's wife did... since looking back indicates nothing but a sense of regret and the thought of worldly life once more." *Life of Anthony, 20*

Saint Anthony yielded his whole life to the commandment of the Lord which says: "He who loses his life for My sake will find it (Matt 10:39)." From the very beginning, he sacrificed himself completely to God and thus performed all his ascetic works for God, not himself.

He no longer desired anything for himself, for he gave himself to God, and so his soul lived for God and was dead to himself and the world. He struggled not so that he could attain a certain level of sanctity, neither in his own eyes nor the eyes of others. His life no longer belonged to him that he might add to it or enhance it, but instead he was gratified in obeying the Lord's commands, those which he had kept till his very last breath.

St. Anthony exceedingly tired himself in prayer and severe asceticism in order to keep his body, heart and mind undisturbed. His goal was not to reach an advanced spiritual state, but so that he could please God with his life, remain obedient to His statutes, and be submissive to His will. In other words, he desired to keep the life he had offered to God pure and without blemish, so that the Lord may receive it from him as an offering of love:

"For chastening the soul renders it as perfect as it was originally when first created…So since we have received the soul as an endowment from God, let us therefore keep it unblemished by tainted thoughts, that it may be recognisable once more by its Creator!" *Life of Anthony, 21*

Hence the tribulations, adversities and misfortunes that befell him, by way of nature, or wicked men or even demons, were of no concern to St. Anthony, nor did they ever cause him to grumble, question or grieve.   Does not his life now belong to God? Is not God now free to do with it what He wills? Isn't he simply required to surrender to the acts of God and His Divine wisdom? St. Anthony did not anticipate reward for enduring hardships and calamities, since his life belonged to the Lord; neither was he awaiting an end for his tribulations and trials, since he did not seek his own comfort, for that too was also God's to decide!

Hence we may define two chief principles in the ascetic life of St. Anthony:

1. Unreserved obedience to the commands of the Lord Jesus, without any additional goal or motive.

2. Complete submission of his life to God, and strictly performing all ascetic worship to offering this life untainted to the Lord. As such we can exclude from the ascetic life upheld by St. Anthony two seriously skewed aspiration that have long corrupted the ascetic life:

1. Making ascetic worship a goal in itself.

2. Struggling in ascetic practices to attain higher gifts or rewards.

The first corrupts the meaning of the Lord's command, and the second demotes ascetic life from being an offering of love and faith.

Anthony's Life is a Perpetuation of the Pentecostal Fire

"That great fiery Spirit which I received, you also receive. And if you wish to receive this Spirit unto yourselves, offer first the labours of the body and meekness of heart, and raise your thoughts to heaven by night and day, and entreat for this fiery Spirit with uprightness of heart and you shall receive Him...And do not doubt in your hearts or be of two hearts and say 'Who can receive this Spirit?' No my children, do not allow these thoughts to enter your hearts, but entreat with sincerity and you shall receive it. I am your father, I toil with you and beseech on your behalf that you may receive this Spirit, for I am certain that you are perfect and able to receive it. For whoever betters himself in this way (that is biblical asceticism), will be given the Spirit from generation to generation and forevermore. Persist in entreating with diligence and it shall be given to you; for this Spirit dwells in the upright of heart. And when you receive this Spirit, heavenly mysteries shall be revealed to you as well as other inexpressible things which I cannot speak of...And you shall have heavenly joy by night and day, and be as those who are in heaven whilst still in the flesh...And no longer shall you pray for yourselves only, but for others also. For everyone who receives this Spirit is able to pray for others...And my petition now for you by night and day is that this great Spirit may dwell in you, this which all the righteous ones have received"

Letter 8

"And they all continued with one accord in prayer and supplication" *Acts 1:14*

TWO SIGNIFICANT EVENTS IN THE HISTORY OF THE CHURCH:

The First is the descent of the Holy Spirit on the apostles who were gathered on the Day of Pentecost, according to God's promise. The second is the founding of monasticism in the Church.

At first, it may seem that there is hardly a connection between the two, but if we look back to the circumstances, reasons and consequences that accompanied each, we may come to realise that we can neatly tie the two events, thus revealing a single continuous event.

The power of witnessing to Christ, from Judea to the ends of the world, was based on the descent of the Holy Spirit. As for the immediate influence on the believers, this was in the form of an abrupt change toward the establishment of a communal life, thus making the individual family as one within the body of the church; individual assets and possessions were sold, and the proceeds given openly to the apostles. Consequently, or perhaps this was in fact the motive, life was entirely consecrated for the service of the church, and this was the formation of the early church; a group of voluntarily deprived, consecrated believers, living a communal life.

Hence if we contemplate on what has happened, it is astounding how money and possession-loving Jews, who greatly valued trade, profit and personal credit, were able to forego, sell and lay down all their possessions at the feet of the apostles. In an instant they accepted to become underprivileged poor!

In addition to material wealth, they were also willing to give up the traditional family entitiy with all its associated Jewish traditions. Concern with tribes, preserving lineage, the sovereignty of the father and the right of inheritance to the firstborn, were all dissipated with the new church structure. This new structure brought with it a new model of fatherhood, a new spiritual lineage were all are brothers, and earthly inheritance is replaced by hope in the things which are not seen.

If we contemplate on all of this, we realise that it was the work of a power superior to the human nature, this which Christ bestowed ten days after his ascension in the person of the Holy Spirit: "But you shall receive power when the Holy Spirit has come upon you" *Acts 1:8*

So now we ought to know that the very first work of this new spiritual power which the believers received was the deep rooted transformation of human nature, transforming its affiliation with money, family and worldly social organisations. And which nature exactly? The stubborn Jewish nature, that previously exhausted all of God's means for spiritual improvement: whether by love, affection, security and a multitude of earthly blessings, or by witnessed miracles, austerity, sternness, exile and misfortune. These means were all unable to promote the Jewish nature even one step further toward sincere spiritual conduct.

When this nature was made subject to the Holy Spirit, instantaneously it became an astounding example of modesty, sincerity, and consecration of body, heart and mind to God.

However, what we would like to contemplate on thoroughly is the state of the early church. What transpired following the Day of Pentecost was initiated by the work of the Holy Spirit in the hearts of the believers. The structure of the early church was formed without any human planning or direction. As the Holy Spirit initially worked in the hearts of believers, each person that accepted the work of the Holy Spirit sold everything they owned, including themselves, to become a member of the church.

The notion of becoming a member of the early church meant that an individual would forego all their possessions, and even their own family, because if a father, mother, brother, sister, son or daughter refused to join the faith, an individual was required to abandon them and everything else and join the church by themselves. The church as a result had become akin to Christ himself, "...See, we have left all and followed you" (Matt 27:19), for the Holy Spirit was secretly abiding amidst the group of believers.

This initial movement that the Holy Spirit prompted in the hearts of the simple believers is a replication of that which Christ himself steered in the hearts of his disciples: Complete abandonment of the world, leaving all things behind and following God.

The church was unable to retain this social and financial arrangement. Nevertheless, this early church model led by the guidance of the Spirit, was only a prelude of the age to come, as a pleasant representation of the kingdom of heaven, where one lives under the complete rule of God, and His ultimate governance.

It was unfortunate for the church to lose this wonderful initial heavenly model, and that the hearts of believers become desensitised to this reaction to heaven's calling through complete abandonment and utter desertion of the world. This portrait in its own right is considered one of the prime works of the Holy Spirit, and is a testimony to the Lord Jesus, an enduring fulfilment of the teachings of the gospel.

However, the Spirit remained working in the hearts of believers in order to achieve this same response toward complete abandonment, sheer self-denial and desertion of the world, but on an individual scale. This was no less in strength or testimony than the initial general movement, and so came about through the magnificent accounts of martyrdom. The martyrs exemplified the continuation of the work of the Holy Spirit, which abundantly filled the hearts of believers, and declared the power of abandonment and utter self-denial alive in the heart of the church. This lead to multiple examples of a genuine response to the call to abandon everything entirely and overcome the world by faith in that which an eye has not seen!

The era of martyrdom had not yet finished before a new response to the exact same call of the Holy Spirit had begun in a different manner; one that was virtually identical to martyrdom, except it was practiced daily and during the course of an entire life! This of course refers to monasticism, which is a complete desertion of everything and carrying the cross daily. Nevertheless if we consider the matter objectively, we find that monasticism is merely a response to the simple flicker of faith that is driven by the hidden flare of the Holy Spirit and so one leaves everything behind, and surges alone to fulfil his faith, hope and love for God.

Hence we have seen that faith during the time of the early church began in this exact same way; leaving everything behind, selling all possessions, forsaking all things, even family members, in order to become a consecrated church member, or more accurately to follow God. We have also seen this in martyrdom, but in a more abrupt fashion. Monasticism then is a continuation of the early faith without alteration. And so we come to read this exact same meaning in the account of St. Anthony:

"And one day as he was going to the Lord's house, Anthony pondered how the apostles left everything and followed the Saviour, and how the book of Acts mentions those who sold their possessions and brought the proceeds and laid them at the apostles' feet."

Hence, the blaze that broke out in the heart of Anthony was a perpetuation of that which dwelt in the heart of the early church starting on the day of Pentecost. Monasticism is actually the unextinguished work of the Holy Spirit that began on the day of Pentecost by forsaking the world, thus establishing the first church. It then became ablaze during the era of martyrdom and so emphasized its strength of faith. Finally it resides in monasticism, consoling the church by the warmth of the apostolic faith which is built on utter desertion and abandonment of the world. Therefore we can say that monasticism has reignited the fire of the Holy Spirit reviving the church till the end of time.

When the Holy Spirit descended on the day of Pentecost, the church went into a state of spiritual ecstasy, reaching a level of realisation in all Divine gifts, as much as the human nature was able to experience. We read in the book of Acts: "Men of Israel, why do you marvel at this? Or why look so intently at us, as though by our own power or godliness we had made this man walk? The God of Abraham, Isaac, and Jacob, the God of our fathers, glorified His Servant Jesus... and through faith in His name, this man was made strong, whom you see and know. Yes, the faith which comes through

Him, has given him this perfect soundness in the presence of you all." (Acts 3:12-16)

Signs and wonders as such remained the focal point of testimony and preaching until the era of martyrdom, where preaching the gospel, and witnessing to Christ began to take place without miracles. Instead, there was a power above miracles, above familial bonds, above the world and its threats, above human nature and its observance of fear and death, and above all existence that is on earth.

This power could be found in the scene of someone, who despite being new to the faith, was able to endure public humiliation, torture and eventually death for Christ's sake. The martyrs' death for the name of Christ became the most vivid representation of the meaning of faith in Jesus Christ and its strength. This alone was sufficient to make bystanders believe in the Lord Jesus. Furthermore, the rulers and those who performed the acts of torture would often tremble and believe themselves. How can any person hold themselves together at the sight of mother Dolagy, as she presents her four young children to be slaughtered, cheering them on to be martyred? She is then taken herself by the sword, all for the love of Christ!

Consequently, martyrdom became another focal point around which preaching the gospel and witnessing to Christ revolved. This power was not an outright miracle, as it was not altogether separate from the human nature, as for instance the healing of the lame man or the raising up of 'Tabitha'. These were not due to a power from within Peter, but rather a power external to him, which Peter called on through faith, supplication and prayer. As for martyrdom, its power resembles that of a miracle exactly, but one that is unified with the human nature.

The martyr receives the exact same power of a miracle, but in his own nature, thus making it a power that is in him, which testifies of the life to come. The effect of this on observers is not to heal their physical ailments, but rather their unbelief. Here the martyr receives from the Holy Spirit power, and a miracle that he declares in himself, one that he puts himself to death with, in order to raise those around him. The martyr compares – before himself, God and others – death for Christ and life without Christ, witnessing boldly that 'For me to live is Christ, and to die is gain' (Philippians 1:21)

The martyr by the strength of his testimony, declares a faith that has been entrenched within him, and a divine strength that is united to his nature. The value of this strength is made clear at the shedding of blood of the martyr, personifying their testimony for the sake of the gospel.

Thus if signs and miracles in the early era were considered a gospel read from beyond the human nature, then martyrdom in the following era became a gospel that is read from within the human nature: a combined divine-human act that is above and united to the human nature.

Therefore, testimony of Christ, the Gospel, and eternal life advanced to the world with great precision. First by the power of wonders, like raising a dead person, in order to show the power of God, which is in its own right a power above death and above human nature. Secondly, by the power of martyrdom: namely by gladly and joyfully accepting death, due to the acceptance of the power of eternal life and its effect on the human nature, raising human nature above itself in an instant through unparalleled faith, a power that valiantly defied and conquered death.

In the Third, we encounter the realm of monasticism. This is the third level of testimony of Christ, the Gospel, and eternal life against this passing world, through the acceptance of power from God. This is, by the work of the Holy Spirit, to utterly desert the world, and transform human nature from its natural state, which is dead by sin, to a state that is beyond its natural form, which is alive by grace. It then remains in this extraordinary state as a sacrifice of love, and an eternal testament to the Divine power that the individual has accepted in him.

Consequently, monastic life encompasses the two previous acts of the Holy Spirit: the act of the miracle by raising a dead person, and the act of martyrdom which elevates the human nature above itself. Furthermore the Holy Spirit adds to both the alibility to continually remain in this state of being transformed from death to life every day, whilst sustaining this elevated form of human nature.

A monk is therefore a Christian who has died, yet rose to life, testifying of the true resurrection for the rest of his days. He is the recipient of an extraordinary living act in his dead nature, which is the aroma of eternal life, and thus is martyred, gladly, every day:

"And when martyrdom ceased, following Peter the seal of martyrs receiving his crown, Anthony departed Alexandria and returned to his solitude, where he sacrificed himself as a martyr every day, to appease his conscience, fighting the hidden battles of faith, as he practiced asceticism with exceeding zeal."

Hence a monk is a genuine representation of the early faith, a living act of the Holy Spirit which began as tongues of fire on the Day of Pentecost passing through the era of martyrdom, being declared by the blood of the martyrs, and overcoming worldly desires.

Monasticism is the final phase of testifying to the fervent and blazing Christian faith, which rested in the Church by the work of the Holy Spirit. It is not a unique kind of faith, or a certain degree of perfection, but a living testimony to the Christian belief, which brings back to mind the early reaction to faith when the Holy Spirit descended on the Day of Pentecost. The core of this reaction was when every person left behind all their possessions, family, and home and joined the apostles – as per the Lords commandment anyway! Monasticism also represents, or brings back to mind, the response of believers to martyrdom, when witnessing to Christ necessitated bearing the cross and being publicly executed.

Thus monasticism is a genuine depiction of the early church's belief and way of life. It is a true model of Christianity exactly in accordance with the teachings of the Bible: Not a later development, but an accurate model of genuine Christian living! Therefore, when we speak of monasticism, we speak of genuine Christian life, and when we speak of genuine Christianity, we speak of monasticism as a living and contemporary model of that life!

The Writings of St. Anthony

If we were to liken St Pachomious, in relation to the monastic order , to Moses who transcribed the old canon, then St. Anthony holds the position of Abraham as forefather of all the fathers. Unfortunately however, despite St. Anthony passing down monasticism as a blessed heritage which has enriched the church for numerous centuries, only some of his writings have survived.

All that is known to the world about the writings of St. Anthony can be summed up in the following:

FIRST:

His blessed biography which was written by St. Athanasius the Apostolic at the request of various monks in the west. It is well known that there were only novice monks in the West (Italy and France) during this time who were in contact with St. Athanasius after his exile to the region. The time of writing the letter – which contained the biography of St. Anthony – was specifically the year 357AD, one year following the departure of the blessed saint in the year 356AD.

From the letter we are able to determine that St. Athanasius did not get the opportunity to elaborate on St. Anthony's life or his sayings to his disciples, being content in only recording some of his own special memories and a few well documented sayings that are mentioned in the letter.

However, in spite of this, the letter has become the most valuable document in the world on monasticism, and on asceticism in general. Especially given that its author is an honourable world renowned and highly spiritual figure. And in fact as soon as the letter emerged in the west, it had an overwhelming influence. It is sufficient, by way of pointing out the tremendous impact which the letter had, to consider the testimony of St Augustine in his confessions (6, 8 & 14) and how much of an impact it had on his conversion and acceptance of the monastic life. The influence of the letter was propagated further by St. Jerome, who translated the letter to Latin around 375AD. It became even more renowned and spread further still, even all the way to Spain.

SECOND:

A handful of letters that he wrote in order to communicate with the monasteries that were under his guidance are also in extant. These include letters to the group of monasteries in Al-Fayom (Al-Naqlon), and the monasteries of Pispir, which were 50 miles south of Cairo to the Nile's east and under the direction of Amathas and Macarious the disciples of St. Anthony. There are also letters to the monasteries of Netria south of Alexandria which were led by St Ammon, St. Anthony's friend. These letters are divided into two groups:

1 – A group that researchers have confirmed is genuine, and were in fact written by St. Anthony. Namely seven letters that can still be found in their original Greek and Latin manuscripts, some in Coptic, some in Syrian and all in Arabic. They are preserved in the Patrologia Greeka Collection, under number (Migne, PG XI, 977-1000). St Jerome mentioned these seven letters: (De Vir. Ill. 88) stating: "He has read and marvelled at their apostolic grounding and strength of instruction".

2 – Another group which is most likely not the authentic work of Saint Anthony. It is presumed that St. Ammon, St. Anthony's disciple and his successor, is the true author of

these letters, and they amount to thirteen letters.

However, after personally reviewing all twenty letters attributed to St. Anthony, carefully revising their spiritual concepts, and comparing the letters to the biography written by St Athanasius, we can safely say that the spirit which produced the teachings and principles is one and the same in all the letters, and that the coherence in style and expression is virtually identical. As for the validity and genuineness of the principles discussed, and also their strength and depth, they undoubtedly point to the character of St. Anthony.

And if we were to concede to what the experts are suggesting, that they are indeed the work of St Ammon, St. Anthony's disciple, it is well known that Ammon was a virtuous character who had many sound sayings in the 'Paradise of the Fathers', and indeed inherited all of his mentor's spirituality. In support of the soundness of his teachings, it is sufficient to consider that St. Anthony, after his departure, entrusted to him managing the affairs of the monks in Pispir who were his most cherished disciples. He also appointed him as father to all his children.

These twenty letters , including what is attributed to Ammon, comprise a great deal of ascetic and hermit tradition, considered by researchers to be at the heart of Eastern asceticism and solitary life in all its forms. As Eperts confirm that the ascetic principles contained therein are of great soundness and strength or in his words: "They preach a solid and healthy asceticism."

As for the ascetic principles in the letters, according to researchers, they are completely void of any 'Oregonic Influences' , which further cements the genuine spirit of asceticism at the time of St. Anthony, before being developed by Evagrius of Pontius, and published across the east in the form of ascetic guidelines.

Thus we will view the twenty letters attributed to St. Anthony, as all being produced by St. Anthony himself, until time permits further research.

The Arabic manuscript is quite old in origin, and there is a printed copy in Cairo which dates back to the year 1899AD. Experts originally thought that the Arabic copy had no originals in other languages, except for a single Syriac copy that has been translated to Arabic by the Maronic scholar Abraham Ekshlinisis. But after some investigation we were able to find an abbreviated original for them in the Philokalia Collection. Also after some comparison, we found that the Greek original, and its English translation, were not taken from the Arabic original due to obvious differences in wording and sentence connections, however the origin for both is undoubtedly the Coptic.

Furthermore, we have managed to find an additional Arabic copy of the twenty letters, which differs from the Arabic copy printed in Cairo, due to variations in wording and phrasing which confirm that it was not taken from the Egyptian copy. This copy was printed in Beirut in the year 1899AD by father 'Avram Al-Dirani Al-Maroni'.

We have relied on all these copies in clarifying the texts cited in underlining the fundamental principles of the ascetic life of St. Anthony.

THIRD:

An important but concise letter written by St. Anthony to his disciple 'Theodore' in relation to repentance, is preserved in the Patrologia Collection under number: (Migne PG, XI, 1065), and has been investigated by experts and authenticated as belonging to St. Anthony. This letter has no Arabic translations. As for the letter to 'Babnoda' (Paphnotious, Anthony's disciple) in the Arabic letters collection, number twenty, this letter does not address repentance.

FOURTH:

Several scattered sayings, which number forty-nine in total, that have featured in 'The Sayings of the Fathers', commonly known as:

Apophthegmata Patrum by Annan Ishou. Tr. By Wallis Budge

This is the book which has been put together by the traveling scholar 'Annan Ishou the Syrian' who travelled to the Wilderness of Scetis in Egypt around the year 660AD, directly following the Arab conquest, and visited the monasteries and recorded the sayings of the fathers from Coptic and Syriac scrolls at the time. These sayings number 1341 saying. Annan states that he put together his book by referring to the writings of the Honoured Palladius, in addition to what he himself gathered. It is well known that Palladius recorded the sayings which he heard himself, those he gathered from desert fathers at the time and also those which he found recorded during the year 420AD.

FIFTH:

Some scattered sayings, which amount to forty brief sayings, which have featured in the collection of sayings

known commonly in Arabic as 'The Paradise of the Fathers' .
According to the scholar 'Butler', the Paradise was translated
to the Arabic from Syriac. It is well known that the Syriac
Manuscript of the Paradise was translated from the Coptic
original in the early sixth century, as confirmed by Wallis
Budge.

Apart from the above mentioned writings which have
been authenticated as being the work of St. Anthony, there
are numerous counterfeit writings that research has shown
to be falsely attributed to St. Anthony. We have reviewed
these writings and found them to be far from the simplistic
monastic spirit, and even peculiar to the early style of the
fathers. Most of these sayings carry an argumentative tone,
which Evagrius and his followers were famous for. They
total 170 saying which featured in the Philokalia Collection,
taken from the Greek original and published in Venice in the
year 1792AD.

As for the contemporary English edition taken from the
Russian translation, this featured a selection of 105 sayings
only.

As a specimen of these sayings, and their style of
writing, there are twenty segments of these discourses that
feature in Arabic, with accompanying monastic instruction,
which are also falsely credited to St. Anthony.

The Fundamental Principles of Asceticism in the life of St. Anthony

1 – The Holy Bible is the underpinning of asceticism.

2 – The Holy Spirit is a companion from beginning to end.

3 – The most dangerous pitfall in ascetic life is regressing backwards.

4 – Asceticism is a life of continual growth.

5 – A wavering heart spoils asceticism.

6 – Discernment is the cornerstone of ascetic life and the measure of all virtues.

7 – Controlling the body is necessary and weakening the body has its limits.

8 – Continuous Repentance through humility and confessing sins is essential.

9 – Spiritual joy is a sign of sound asceticism.

10 – Fervent ascetic labours are an obligation and a grace at the same time!

11 – Ascetic perfection is achieved through diligence, and Christian perfection through Grace, and one does not suffice for the other.

12 – The ascetic tradition of the holy fathers illuminates the way.

We present here a summary of the fundamental ascetic principles in the teachings of St. Anthony, and so by way of highlighting them here in a very clear and concise manner, we hope to draw the attention to the teaching of our Holy Orthodox Church to what these teachings comprise in the way of genuine Biblical teachings, orthodox faith and spiritual depth.

Moreover, we also wish to draw the attention of our Christian brethren from non-orthodox denominations to these profound spiritual teachings, which are set on tremendously concrete biblical grounds. St. Anthony's teachings preach the fervent and zealous work of God's grace that unites with man's work thus making works, grace and grace, works!

St. Anthony is credited for teaching that it is the Holy Spirit who constantly inspires and leads to repentance. He is also recognized for endorsing the necessity for sorrow and remorse of the soul, for the ignorance of its sins, yet he is also credited for the preaching of heavenly joy which fills the soul and overwhelms and engulfs it with blessed hope in a delightful future!

We now present to the entire world these sturdy teachings as a lively testament that the Coptic Orthodox Church is the founder of biblical and evangelical asceticism that is based on the grace and work of the Holy Spirit. This grows and is perfected by Divine revelation and realised by heavenly union.

First Ascetic Principle

Summary: The Bible is the underpinning of asceticism, and in light of the statutes and commands of the bible we learn and practice asceticism from start to end.

Sayings of the Saint :

"The Holy Books suffice for teaching." *Life of Anthony, 16*

"If one armed themselves with steadfast zeal toward the commandments of God, the Holy Spirit will istruct them on how to cleanse their spirit and body" *Letters, 1*

"Therefore know my children that all statutes are neither burdensome nor wearing, but rather a source of true light and everlasting joy to those that follow them." *Letters, 14*

"A brother asked St. Anthony: "Which commandment should I keep in order to please God? He replied: "Set the Lord constantly before your eyes, at all times, and everywhere you go. And before any task, recite a section from the Holy Books that your works may be blessed." *Sayings, 35*

"For I know that, whoever knows what is written *in the Bible*, knows God, and whoever knows God, discerns the work of God in His creation." *Letters, 3*

"Those who wish to toil in a life of asceticism in Jesus Christ must reject all bodily lusts imploring the Lord Jesus, who through His mercy and compassion, will vanquish all the temptations and tribulations of the body." *Letters, 4*

"A group of brothers approached St. Anthony and asked him: "How can we attain our salvation?"

He said to them: "Have you heard what the Lord says?"

They said: "From your mouth, O father."

He said to them: "Whoever slaps you on your right cheek, turn the other to him also." (A primary ascetic principal)

They replied: "We cannot bear this!"

So he said to them: "Then endure only the first slap." (A lesser ascetic principal)

They replied: "This also we cannot do!"

He said to them: "So then do not repay evil to those who spitefully accuse you." (Yet an even lesser ascetic principal)

They replied: "Yet this also we cannot do!!"

So the Saint called his disciple and said to him: "Prepare a meal for them and then send them on their way for they are ill; this they cannot endure, and that they cannot perform, and the edicts of the Lord they do not wish to keep, what more then, can I do for them?" *Paradise of the Fathers, 8*

"St. Anthony was questioned on the meaning of the Apostle's proverb: "Rejoice in the Lord always"

So he replied: If we delight in keeping the Lord's commandments, then this is rejoicing in the Lord. Thus let us rejoice in keeping the commandments of the Lord, and in the success of our brethren, and keep ourselves from worldly joys and pleasures, if we wish to be our God's elect."

Paradise of the Fathers, 10

"St. Anthony was asked about the meaning of the verse "Love your neighbour as yourself".

He replied: Man's life and death hinge on his neighbour, thus if we do well to our neighbours we gain and profit ourselves! But if we resent them, we are in fact resenting God!" *Sayings, 33*

"Children, do not leave a dwelling place within yourselves for Satan, so that God's wrath doesn't settle upon you and the evil ones make a mockery you, thus hold firm to these words of mine, because they know that our lives are in one another...For he who loves his brother loves God – for we are all members of one body whose head is Christ – and he who loves God cherishes his own soul!" *Letters, 6*

Second Ascetic Principle

Summary: The Holy Spirit calls a person to repentance, and if they respond He motivates, enlightens and facilitates the way of righteousness. When the person toils and labors, the Holy Spirit works to sanctify them, till they yield Godly fruits.

SAYINGS OF THE SAINT:

"The Holy Spirit who provokes repentance is also the one who leads the repentant to perform spiritual deeds"

I perceive that the grace of the Holy Spirit is of utmost readiness to fill those who approach spiritual deeds with the fullness of their hearts and have insisted firmly to remain steadfast on the path of righteousness.

The Holy Spirit who called them, eases their way from the start, and makes the works of repentance enjoyable and a relief.

Finally, the Holy Spirit truthfully reveals to them all the works of repentance, and fills them with holy zeal.

The Spirit indicates to them what they ought to know, and sets for them boundaries in all things related to body and soul, that they may be led by the Spirit to perfect transformation toward God their Creator.

Thus to this end, the Spirit continually entice them to devote their entire spiritual and bodily effort, that the two may become sanctified together, and deemed worthy to inherit the eternal kingdom.

And so the Spirit drives the body toward persevering in fasting, service and many vigils. As for the soul, it is driven toward eagerness and obedient persistence to every work that serves the body, without neglect but with the fear of God...until it prospers and bears the fruit!" *Letters 1*

"If the soul becomes armed with unceasing endurance in God's testimonies (His statutes and promises), then the Holy Spirit directs the mind to (the means of) purifying both body and soul from all inclinations (which lure toward sin). However if one strays from these testimonies and teachings, they will be overcome by the allures of the enemy and become defiled by them. However, if the soul returns and adheres to the spirit of salvation, then one will realise that persevering for the sake of God is their true source of rest and tranquillity.

The sayings I have taught are so that your bodies and souls become united in repentance, accordingly if the mind gains this grace, then one will ask through the Holy Spirit, who begins to expel from the soul the dreads that have befallen it due to the (natural) lusts of the flesh.

If the Holy Spirit is in unison with the mind, through the observance of the divine commandments, He guides ousting the infirmities of sin from the soul one after the other.

The Holy Spirit is a refuge and a shelter unto him (the struggling ascetic), augments him with strength, and douses from him all evil set upon him.

The heart that has become entrenched with grace, controls the members and moves them as per the will of the

Holy Spirit inperforming righteous deeds, so that the body is made perfect in all virtues and returns to the dominion of the Holy Spirit." *Letters, 1*

"Therefore I do not grow weary of entreating the Lord for you that you may come to recognise the grace which is set before you, for God warns everyone through the workings of His Divine Grace. Therefore do not cease or give up beseeching the Father's goodness, until he bestows on you grace from above in order to learn what is required of you.

Whoever despises the lusts of this materialistic world and lifts up his heart toward God, God will have pity on him and grant him the imperceptible fire of the Spirit to scorch all his infirmities and sanctify his thoughts, and so the Holy Spirit shall accompany him and dwell within him, thus he will be able to worship the Father appropriately (in spirit and truth). But, if we continue to be in accord with this world's fleeting and materialistic desires we will remain adversaries of God, His holy angels and the choir of His Saints!" (Letter 5)

"You have been counted worthy of blessing because of the Grace bestowed upon you, however you must not become idle in your battle for the Lord, who has visited you and dawned on you from above that you may become a blessed and holy sacrifice to him." (Letter 6)

Third Ascetic Principle

Summary: The most dangerous pitfall in ascetic life is regressing backwards. Boredom is an example of this.

SAYINGS OF THE SAINT:

"Take heed not to regress backwards, once you have begun. Or that your resolves decline in times of tribulation.

And do not say we have long lived in asceticism, but rather let us grow even more zealous as though we're just starting out every day (St. Anthony considers himself here as a beginner), because indeed life is too short when compared to eternity!

Therefore my children we must not grow weary or count the days too long.

Therefore my children we must remain steadfast in our asceticism and not slumber, for God himself works with us in our struggles as it is written "now He who searches the hearts knows what the mind of the Spirit is, because He makes intercession for the saints according to the will of God." (Romans 8:27)

In order for us to avoid laziness and negligence, we should remember the words of the apostle: "I die daily" (1 Cor 15:31), and thus if we live each day as though we are being put to death we will not stumble.

One must not regress or look back, since this only indicates a sense of regret and the thought of worldly life once more." *Life of Anthony, 16-20*

"The Spirit that guides the repentant grants him special comfort and persuades him not to turn back and mingle with the things pertaining to this world. The spirit turns the attention of the soul toward this purpose that it may come to behold the splendor of the purity, which the soul will attain through the work of repentance." *Letters, 1*

"Know that by your patience, you subdue the power of the enemy." *Letters, 7*

Fourth Ascetic Principle

Summary: Asceticism is a life of continual growth toward a predetermined goal set by the Holy Spirit for our lives. It is essential that we continue to increase our struggle in accordance with the objectives set for us by the Holy Spirit.

SAYINGS OF THE SAINT:

"Since we have begun walking the path of righteousness earnestly, we must therefore intensify our struggle, so that we may attain the virtues that are set (by the Holy Spirit) before us." *Life of Anthony, 20*

"The Lord guides everyone through the work of His Grace, therefore do not slumber or grow weary, and pray by night and day that God may grant you heavenly support and guide you toward what you ought to do.

If the heavenly saints behold in us earnestness in growing spiritually and presenting ourselves to God, they shall not cease supplicating for us before the Creator.

Whoever does so, God will have pity on him and grant him the invisible fire of the Spirit to scorch all his infirmities (the infirmities of sin) and sanctify his thoughts, and so the Holy Spirit will dwell within him." *Letters, 5*

"For whoever betters himself in this way, will be given the Spirit from generation to generation and forevermore.

I know of some who received the Spirit, and because they could not persist, the Spirit did not abide in them."

Letters, 8

"I do not grow weary of remembering you in my supplication before God by night and by day so that your devotion to God may be firm; and thus your virtues may be multiplied, your gaze fixed and your discernment prudent and God shall grant you tremendous power moreover." *Letters, 12*

"I continually entreat my God for you that the works of the Holy Spirit may grow within you, and that God may reveal to you the greatness of His mysteries.

My supplication at all times is for you to be made perfect, that you may come to know the abundance of the kingdom of God." *Letters, 13*

"Beloved know this, a true ascetic is held by nothing, for asceticism in its fullness is being entirely unbound by any evil act. Whoever is yet chained to any evil doing is a long way from perfection."

Whoever aspires to live the ascetic way must envy Joseph's purity and chastity, discipline himself, and overcome all evil lusts." (Letter 17)

"You cannot progress or develop if you do not heed your spiritual father's instruction…For our fathers did so themselves, and so because they kept the instruction of their fathers before them, they progressed and became mentors." *Letter, 18*

Fifth Ascetic Principle

Summary: Asceticism can be spoiled due to a divided and wavering heart, pretence, hypocrisy and hardness of heart.

SAYINGS OF THE SAINT:

"I write to you this letter my blessed children, so you may know that those who love God and seek him with all their hearts, God hears them and grants their requests. As for those who do not come to Him with all their hearts and their works are done in pretence before men so that they may be glorified by them, to those He hears not and their appeals are rejected, and they are despised by God for their hypocrisy.

For this reason the power of God does not work in them for their faintness of heart in all that they do. Hence they cannot perceive the splendour of God nor His joy, and the works of God become burdensome for them like a heavy load.

As for you my beloved, when you offer the fruits of your labours before God, endeavor to evade the spirit of vainglory, so that God may accept your fruits and you may receive from Him the power which is given to the elect.

As for those whom the devil shares in their deeds, he spoils their fruits for they attain their virtues accompanied by desire for the vain glory of men. They appear to men as having fruits (due to their works and virtues), but they do not, and God forsakes them to waste away, like a fig tree that has withered." *Letters, 10*

"All those whose fruits are dead, are not counted in God's inheritance, but rather He blames them saying: even if your necks become bent like a ring (because of deprivation and humility), you are clothed in sackcloth (garment of repentance) and your heads covered in ashes, all this I have rejected! For you perform the will of your wicked hearts and oppress those who are under your authority.

Children, these are dead fruits (deceptive labours), and those that perform them God hears not their supplications." *Letters, 15*

Sixth Ascetic Principle

Summary: Discernment (differentiating between right and wrong) is the cornerstone of ascetic life and the measure of all virtues.

SAYINGS OF THE SAINT:

"Indeed all virtues are useful and necessary for those who seek God and wish to get closer to Him, however many have exhausted themselves in severe fasts, vigils, solitude and abstinence, yet they have strayed from the right path because they did not have the spirit of discernment. Discernment directs a person to the true path and steers him away from treacherous ways. It prevents one from being robbed from the right due to self-righteousness and from the left by idleness and weariness." *Paradise of the Fathers, 13*

"I do not grow weary in my supplications for you by night and by day, so that the Lord may enlighten your hearts to realize the cunningness and wickedness of the devils, and that He may grant you a watchful heart and the spirit of discernment, so that you may raise your souls up as pure living sacrifices, and recognise Satan's evil counsel.

For they (devils) induce us to speak evil of one another, praise ourselves, judge others, say pleasant things whilst our hearts are bitter, contend and resist to defend our words so that we remain dignified, and commit to works we cannot endure. They keep from us those things which are in our interest and turn them against us and they persuade us to be joyful in times of sorrow and weep in times of laughter, and thus at all times they yearn for us to stray from the right way.

Therefore we ought to comprehend the traps of the enemy and avoid them, because the sins and iniquities they entice us with are hidden, and so we accept their obscure thoughts and consequently they become deeds in our flesh." *Letters, 6*

Those who have trained their senses and by way of constant examination, God grants vision and discernment in everything they do, so that neither devils nor men can use righteous deeds to misguide them.

True vision, which is discernment, is surpassed by nothing in the Christian faith…Those who attain it do not toil in vain and to them nothing is impossible, and thus the Joy of our Lord consoles them night and day.

Therefore implore the Lord for the spirit of discernment with tears by night and by day, so that you may abound in every good thing and become more splendid in all that you do. In this way you may attain perfection." *Letters, 11*

Seventh Ascetic Principle

Summary: Controlling the body and governing its desires is an essential necessity in ascetic struggle, meanwhile weakening the body has limits.

SAYINGS OF THE SAINT:

"Truly my children, everyone who battles must first conquer the desires of the body, which arise due to excessive eating and drinking, only then can he gird himself with purity and sooth his heart with the words of the psalm: "Gird your sword upon your thigh, O mighty one" (Ps 45:3). This sword is the might of the word of God which is given to the chaste; this is the sword that pierces all evil desires.

And also Jacob, the Angel of the Lord wrestled with him and struck his thigh, and so his strength waned and his body was weakened and he was called Israel, that is; 'Beholder of God'. We also therefore must weaken the body wisely and with care, in order to weaken the desires of the body and lessen their ferocity, because the weakening of the body accomplishes within us the strength of purity...For if the body is weakened the spirit is strengthened. Let us thus weaken our bodies wisely in order to assert control over our souls and behold God!

For if we deprive the body and subject it to the spirit, bodily thoughts that are the cause of enmity with God dwindle and perish, and so the soul shines and becomes a temple for the Holy Spirit.

Thus whoever struggles to purify all his members (mind, heart, desire and body), is the true ascetic." *Letters, 17*

"St. Anthony spent almost twenty years alone practising his ascetic discipline this way, neither going out, nor being often seen by anyone. The first time that he came out of the barracks and appeared before those who came to see him, they were amazed to see that his body had maintained its natural condition; being neither fat from lack of exercise nor weakened from fasting. They found him just as they had known him before his withdrawal!" *Life of Anthony, 14*

Eighth Ascetic Principle

Summary: Humility and continual repentance through confessing of sins and lamentation on past ignorance

regardless of spiritual advancement – is necessary in order to prevent regression. This is the Lord's will.

Although a repentant individual has utter confidence in the ultimate redemptive power of Christ's blood and that God has absolved him of his sins and bore the penalty of his trespasses, he should not forgive himself or absolve his own conscience as though he has not sinned at all

SAYINGS OF THE SAINT:

"Declare always that you are sinners and mourn your ignorant deeds, in this way the will of God shall abide within you, and work with you. For God is beneficent and forgives the trespasses of all those who return to Him, and no longer recalls their sins. However God desires us to recount our own sins, lest we forget them and become accountable once more for what has been forgiven to us. This is what befell the servant who was forgiven his debt by his master. When he disregarded his master's forgiveness and demanded from his follow servant the debt which was owed to him, his master pursued his debt once more, after it was forgiven.

Therefore we ought to always remember the sins that God has forgiven us; furthermore we ought to never forget them so that God may look upon our meekness and lowly state as debtors!

David, when God granted him forgiveness of his sin, did not overlook nor forget it himself, but instead he recorded it in Psalm 51, as an everlasting testimony from generation to generation: "My sin is ever before me."

Therefore, a sinner whose sins have been forgiven by God should always remember them himself, so that he may find favour in the sight of the Lord.For thus the Lord spoke on the mouth of Jeremiah the prophet: "For I am merciful says the Lord, and I have lifted my wrath away from you, nevertheless you ought to know your own wickedness."

We too, my children, when the Lord blots out our transgressions, should not absolve ourselves of our own sins, but always recall them through the renewal of repentance... This I bring to your attention my beloved as I am aware of your great virtues, and recall it to you lest you slumber and your light fades and so that you may bring forth even better fruits worthy of the heavenly monastic way." (Letter 16)

"Thus all those who desire to return once more to their first rank, cannot do so except by humility, that is why, without great humility in your whole heart, mind, spirit, soul and body you will not be able to inherit the Kingdom of God.

Truly, my children in the Lord, I ask my Creator night and day, from whom I have the pledge of His Spirit (2 Cor 1:22), to open for you the eyes of your hearts to perceive your own confusion. For him who knows his own shame, seeks again his elect grace, and whoever knows his own death, also knows his eternal life!" *Letters, 6*

"Take heed not to be of a weary heart, for a weary heart brings about (detrimental) grief." *Paradise of the Fathers, 13*

Ninth Ascetic Principle

Summary: Spiritual joy is the power of asceticism and a sign of its soundness, for it nurtures the soul and elevates the mind and nourishes it. Spiritual joy is an incentive for persevering in struggle and conquers Satan and all his evil traps. Hence spiritual joy stemming from a blessed present and a triumphant future assures the strength and success of repentance.

Sayings of the Saint:

"For just as trees do not grow unless the element of water is available to them, so also the soul cannot mount upwards unless it receives heavenly joy. Subsequently, as for the souls that have received the heavenly joy, they alone are able to ascend into the heights." *Letters, 13*

"Since Godly joy nurtures and nourishes their minds and souls, and raises their spirits to heaven, for as the body is sustained by food and water and the appetite suppressed when an illness befalls the body thus being overcome by the enemy and not returning to full health unless seen by a physician, so too the soul if the joy of God is not abound within it, is found ill and ridden with sinister infirmities (destructive grief). But if the soul earnestly seeks a servant of God, trained in spiritual medicine, he will cure it from its pangs, raise it once more, and prescribe for it what is of God, which is the heavenly joy that is its food and nourishment. It can thus resist its enemies and overcome them, trampling down their wicked thoughts and councils, being made perfect in heavenly joy.

Therefore incline to your fathers and obey them, and you will not stumble. Yet I make known to you another way, which affirms a person from start to end, and that is to love the Lord your God with a full heart and worship Him in truth. If you do this, God will grant you His great power and joy, and so you will relish in the works of God and also all the labours of the body will be pleasing to you." *Letters, 18*

"Let us not allow our resolve to wane, or conjure up cowardly thoughts in our souls, or invent fears for ourselves, saying; 'Oh, I hope that when a demon comes he does not turn me upside down! I hope he does not pick me up and throw me to the ground! Or suddenly come up to me and throw me into confusion!' Let us, not even remotely, dwell on such things.

Let us be all the more courageous and let us always rejoice because we are being saved. Let us reflect in our souls on how the Lord is always with us.

For if the demons find us fearful and distressed, then like thieves, finding the place unguarded, they immediately set upon us and do to us what we have conjured up in our thoughts and much more! If they see us fearful and afraid, they will even more forcefully increase our terror with apparitions and threats, and so the wretched soul is tormented all the more with these illusions.

If, however, they find us rejoicing in the Lord and thinking about the good things to come, they turn away ashamed and confounded.

As a result, if we wish to hold the enemy in contempt, let us keep our thoughts set on the Lord and His work, and let our souls rejoice always in hope." *Life of Anthony, 42*

"The character of his (St. Anthony) soul was pure, for it had neither been contracted by suffering or pleasure, nor had it been afflicted by laughter or sorrow." *Life of Anthony, 14*

Tenth Ascetic Principle

Summary: Fervent labours endured are a biblical and ascetic decree, for they all are entirely the Lord's commandment.

And despite arising out of our own free will, and the essence of our incorruptible being: "O God the Great and the Eternal, who formed man in incorruption" (St Basil's Liturgy – Prayer of Reconciliation), nonetheless after the gift of Holy Baptism, our labours become united with the power and fire of the Holy Spirit. Thus being able by this newly formed nature to scorch sins and iniquities, we are obliged to uphold them in our novel Christian life but at the same time count their results as being due to the work of the Holy Spirit.

Thus we are judged if we do not perform righteous deeds, for through their fervour we are elevated toward God, however when we are elevated and made Holy, this is in fact not due to our own deeds, but rather due to the work of the Holy Spirit and the fire that has united with our labours!

SAYINGS OF THE SAINT:

"Thus I beseech you brethren in the name of our Lord Jesus Christ, that you may remain steadfast and not overlook your salvation, let each of you tear his heart, rather than his cloak (formerly a sign of repentance), lest we have put on the monastic garb (The 'Eskeem') whilst all the more adding unto ourselves a greater judgement, for each one will be judged according to his deeds." *Letters, 1*

"I think it is no great wonder, if you neglect yourselves and do not discern your works, that you should fall into the hands of the devil. When you think you are near to God, in your expectation of the light, darkness shall overtake you." *Letter, 6*

"I entreat you to comprehend that all the works that we offer up unto God, by the grace bestowed upon us, do not at all come into comparison with His humility for us and on our behalf.

Truly, my children, though we commit ourselves with all power to seek the Lord, what thanks do we deserve? For it is our duty, for we are only seeking what is in our original nature. For every man who seeks God or serves Him, does what is natural. But every sin, of which we are guilty, is foreign and unnatural.

I beseech you therefore, my beloved in the Lord, to rouse up your minds in the fear of God. Let this become clear to you, that John the forerunner of Jesus baptised unto remission of sins for our sake, that we may come to be baptised by fire and the Spirit in Jesus Christ. As for the fire, it is the fire of righteous deeds. Let us now prepare in all holiness to cleanse the senses of our mind that we may be clean by the baptism of Jesus, in order to offer ourselves as sacrifice to God by way of our labours. And His Spirit, the Paraclete, comforts us and guides us to the work of repentance, to recover our unfading inheritance." *Letters, 7*

"If you wish to receive this spirit unto yourselves, offer first the labours of the body and meekness of heart, and raise your thoughts to heaven by night and day, and entreat for this fiery spirit with uprightness of heart and you shall receive it." *Letters, 8*

"The reason for their (the saints) ascent to heaven, was the invisible fire, which is the fire of righteous deeds, that engulfed their hearts.

To what can the soul, within which the fire of God dwells, be likened? It is like a bird with two wings, soaring up into the heavens. Thus the wings of a worshiping soul are the power of the fire of God, which lifts it up above into the heavens.

Thus do not let the power of this fire depart from you, for Satan wages numerous wars in order to hamper this blaze which has been given to you by the Lord, since he knows that he has no power over you so long as this fire is within you.

Satan troubles the soul with numerous plights, in order to quench this spirit of virtue. Foremost among these plights is (the lust of) resting the body along with all the matters of the flesh.

I therefore entreat God for you, so that He may pour into your hearts that fire which Jesus came to send upon the earth (Luke 12:49), that you may be able to exercise your heart and senses, to know how to discern good from evil, right from left, and reality from illusion." *Letters, 3*

"Truly, my children, unless each one of you shall despise all earthly possession, and stretch out the hands of his heart to heaven, to the Father of all, he cannot be saved. But whoever does what I have said, God will have pity on him for his labour, and grant him that invisible fire which will burn up all impurity from him, and sanctify his mind." *Letters, 5*

"But as for you my beloved, strive in order that the

divine power may come upon you and dwell within you, give you fervour and accompany you at all times. And I entreat God for you that this fire may be given to you always, for nothing is more precious on the face of the earth. And if one of you sees that your fervour withdraws and leaves you, seek it earnestly and it will return.

And if, due to your laziness or slumber, you see your heart weighed down temporarily, bring your soul before you and question it until it becomes fervent again and is set on fire in God." *Letters, 10*

"Transform your bodies into censors that offer up your thoughts and inclinations before the Lord, through the raising of your minds and hearts, and beseech him to ignite within you the fire of his love, in order to devour all that is within this censor and purify it. And thus my children, if you attain these virtues, do not perceive that this was through your own doing, but rather know that it was due to the Divine power that works alongside all your deeds." *Letters, 6*

Eleventh Ascetic Principle

Summary: Asceticism is to follow the commandments, and perfect asceticism is to be set free from any kind of evil. However ascetic perfection differs from Christian perfection, as ascetic perfection ends with purity of heart, and thus one is able to see God spiritually, and so Christian perfection, is when we are in perfect union with God.

Therefore ascetic perfection qualifies one for Christian perfection; hence there is no substitute for ascetic struggle.

SAYINGS OF THE SAINT:

"Whoever desires to become perfect through asceticism, should not be a slave to any sin, for he who is bound to even one form of evil is far from perfection. For it is written: "For though I am free from all, I have made myself a servant to all, that I might win the more" (1 Cor 9:19). And thus St Paul – being free from the bondage of sin – was able to be of benefit to many, those who were still bound by sin and iniquities and thus lacked power.

For the Spirit enters not the soul of one whose heart is defiled , nor the body that sins, a Holy power it is, removed from all deceit." *Letters, 4*

"As for the Apostle Paul, he gained (Christian) perfection when the Lord Jesus appeared to him, and from that point on he became an aid (through his ministry and teachings) to those who lacked the power to attain perfection and soar into the heavens.

St Paul, my children, attained perfection because:

First: He was freed from evil (by grace and struggle)

Second: Was not overcome after that by any sort of lust or desire, for he became an ascetic.

Third: Beholding the Lord Jesus set him free. And so after he saw Him he immediately followed His path and commandments and thus attained ultimate perfection and humility.

And so also all those who hold firm to the Lord's commands, they know the truth and the truth sets them free and spares their souls from all evil, as was the case with St. Paul. (St. Anthony here equates knowing the truth, after fulfilling the commandments, to beholding the Lord). Thus, St Paul says of himself: "Am I not free? Have I not seen Jesus Christ our Lord?" (1 Cor 9:1)

Still, many in their ignorance say; 'We have seen the Lord Jesus just like the apostles have', they are lost and have been led astray, for they have no eyes (power) to behold the Lord like the apostle (St. Paul) did, since the apostle beheld him as the disciples did (in His transfiguration). For he beheld him with the eye of his heart and his genuine faith, like the bleeding woman who touched the edge of His garment with great faith and so was immediately healed.

So just like the Lord appeared to his apostle Paul, when he was overcome with afflictions and set him free, likewise everyone who has been spared from his afflictions (sin) will qualify to behold the Lord with the eyes of his heart, for he cannot behold this incredible radiant light, which Paul gazed upon, with the eyes of his body.

Know that, if the spirit of sin dies within a man (that is to say if lustful desires have ceased from him) God appears to the soul and purifies it, along with the body. Whereas if the spirit of sin still abides within a man (lustful desires have not yet ceased), one can never behold the glory of God, because the soul dwells in darkness. It is void of the light that we behold God with: "In Your light we see light" (Psalm 36:9). And what is this light that we see God with? It is the light, which Christ mentions in the Gospel, (the simple eye) of a whole body full of light and nothing dark (void of sin).

The Son, my children, does not reveal His Heavenly Father to those who dwell in darkness, but to those who abide in the light, those who are children of the light, whose hearts' eyes have been illuminated by knowledge of the Divine commandments! For the eyes of the righteous are completely void of iniquity and therein no trace of darkness remains.

If sin and darkness (lustful desires) are present, they prevent the soul from attaining the faultless vision which the righteous possess. This is the vision that St Paul speaks of: "with unveiled face, beholding the glory of the Lord (without sin or darkness)…Are being transformed into the same image from glory to glory" (2 Cor 3:18)…From faith to faith…And from virtue to perfect righteousness. This advancement and progress is what draws us closer to God in order to obtain the ability to behold and know Him. As it is written: "By those who come near Me, I am regarded as Holy" (Lev 10:3). Accordingly if the mind approaches God, it is made Holy, it is united to Him and made one with Him, and so the enemy can by no means draw near it again!

Our teacher St Paul indicates that we ought to sprint toward perfection (the ultimate goal) saying: "I discipline my body and bring it into submission" (1 Cor 9:27). Therefore, so long as we still have time in this body, let us surge forward and attain perfection as this saint did, who said: "I have fought the good fight, I have finished the race, I have kept the faith. Finally, there is laid up for me the crown of righteousness." (2 Tim 4:7, 8). Therefore, you also should likewise do. For he who labours in idleness and laziness shall meet his end before his perfection in Christ!

The days of a soul are like those of the body, passing through childhood, adulthood and old age. These resemble the beginning of faith, struggle and perfection.

Hence, when the soul believes in Christ it is born, as it is written in the Gospel. The Apostle John wrote concerning this birth, indicating its beginning, midpoint and completion: "I write to you, little children, because your sins are forgiven you... I write to you, young men, because you have overcome the wicked one... I write to you, fathers, because you have known Him who is from the beginning!!" (1 John 2: 12, 13).

Thus we find David the prophet, knowing that his days were numbered and that he had not yet reached spiritual perfection, entreat the Lord saying: "O my God, do not take me away in the midst of my days" (Psalm 102:24), since he feared that his life would end before his spiritual days were complete!" *Letters, 17*

"Rest assured that without purity of heart and body, no one can be perfect before God, as it is written; "Blessed are the pure in heart, for they shall see God" (Matt 5:8). Hence perfection is accomplished through purity of heart (because through purity of heart God is revealed!)" *Letters, 20*

"It is mentioned concerning the pure saintly fathers,

that after beholding the Lord, they became even more humble. Thus we hear of righteous Job, who when the eyes of his heart were finally opened and he beheld the Lord, counted himself as dust and ashes…Also Isaiah the prophet after rebuking the people for their sins, saw the Lord and immediately humbled himself declaring; "Woe is me, for I am undone! Because I am a man of unclean lips." (Isaiah 6:5)

And so the saints' great humility is in fact owing to what they have seen of God's glory. Thus the soul attains true humility on earth by beholding – from afar – the glory which it shall receive (undeservedly).

"Many have spent all their days in monasticism and virginity and have not gained the proper and virtuous tuition, for they forsook their fathers' teachings and followed their own inklings… They will perish with the five foolish virgins for they have spent their days in folly and did not control their tongues nor purify their bodies and senses from evil desire nor their hearts from blemish, surely the things that we ought to bitterly weep over… They no longer possess heavenly desires nor do they mourn their souls so that their lamps (their souls) may be lit!

I only write to you seeking the salvation of your souls, and in order to present you as a pure unblemished bride for Christ, Bridegroom to all virtuous souls, as the Apostle Paul says: "I have betrothed you to one husband, that I may present you as a chaste virgin to Christ!" (2 Cor 11:2)]
Letters, 20

Twelfth Ascetic Principle

Summary: Keeping the ascetic tradition and teachings of the holy fathers illuminates the way and leads to true discernment, spiritual advancement and growth. It also leads to knowing God's will, receiving the aid of the heavenly hosts, gaining the blessings of the fathers, and sharing in the luminous eternal inheritance.

SAYINGS OF THE SAINT:

"Truly, my children, my heart is in awe and my spirit in anguish, for each one of us has been given free will to perform the works of the saints, but instead we have become dominated by our own free choice and take our pleasure in sin like drunkards on new wine, and so refuse to raise our minds and seek the glory of heaven, the work of all the saints, and to walk in their footsteps!" *Letters, 5*

"For as such you have sought God, imitating your fathers in faith, so that you should receive the promises also, because you are reckoned their sons; for sons inherit the blessing of their fathers, because their zeal was like theirs. For this cause, since the blessed Jacob followed all the God-fearing ways of his parents, the blessings of his parents came upon him too. And having been blessed by them, he saw the Ladder and angels ascending and descending on it." *Letters, 14*

"I wish to inform you, beloved children, that I have long toiled in the deserts and wilds entreating the Lord night and day to reveal to me his Divine will, but he revealed nothing to me, until I heeded the instructions of my fathers and sought the will of God from them. For he who follows the words of his fathers, to the Lord follows. So therefore my beloved, listen to your father in what I have written to you, so that his blessing may come upon you and you may find rest, grace and strength and the Lord may straighten all your ways." *Letters, 20*

"So therefore my blessed children, incline to what I have said to you: For you cannot progress, mature spiritually, differentiate between good and evil and reach perfection if you do not heed the instructions of your fathers who were consummated in the faith, for our fathers so did in following the teachings of their fathers, and thus progressed, advanced and became instructors."

"Many times did my Master Lord Christ wish to relieve me of the burdens of this body and receive my soul, yet He has left my poor spirit in the flesh for your instruction saying; you are a righteous caretaker and mother, and so I have left you yet a while longer to raise your children well. And so my blessed children accept now my final blessing and here is your father's last decree, so uphold the words therein, for it is your true inheritance."

Close

A moving quote by a layman protestant historian of German birth and American upbringing:

"Indeed Anthony concealed underneath his sheepskin clothing, the spirit of an innocent child (perhaps he wanted to say a lamb), in simplicity and gentleness along with a unique drive and willpower! His fervent love for God remained ablaze for ninety years, despite the absence of all means of comfort and luxuries! He was able to utterly conquer all temptations of the flesh and through virtue alone, without the aid of learning or tuition, Anthony became one of the most famous and influential figures in early Church history!"

Phillip Chaff: History of the Christian Church III, 188

www.ingramcontent.com/pod-product-compliance
Lightning Source LLC
Chambersburg PA
CBHW021911040426
42447CB00007B/807